Fiction

7) E.g. Because her mother had rejected her. (**1 mark**)
8) He showed Tobi how to hold the bottle correctly. (**1 mark**)
9) He made sure she was fed.
He made sure she was clean.
He made sure she had enough love and attention.
(**1 mark for any of the above answers, 2 marks in total**)
10) Tobi had travelled from Birmingham. — True
Tobi had never been to the farm before. — False
The lamb was in the nearest stall to Tobi. — False
Tobi's family stayed on the farm for one week. — True
(**1 mark for all correct**)

Pages 18-19 — Inference Questions

1) E.g. He pinched his nose tight. (**1 mark**)
2) an opinion (**1 mark**)
3) E.g. He realised the holiday might not be so bad because he could watch television. (**1 mark**)
4) He flushed.
He looked down at the ground.
(**1 mark for any of the above answers**)
5) He has a lot to do. (**1 mark**)
6) sorry for it (**1 mark**)
7) He wanted Tobi to like feeding the lamb. (**1 mark**)
8) He punched the air.
He sprinted back to the cottage.
He was "bursting to share the news".
When he spoke to his parents, he talked very quickly.
(**1 mark for any of the above answers**)
9) You can tell they were surprised because their mouths were hanging open. (**1 mark**)
AND
You can tell they were pleased because they smiled. (**1 mark**)

Page 20 — Word Meaning Questions

1) beautiful (**1 mark**)
2) It was loud.
It was high-pitched.
It was irritating.
(**1 mark for any of the above answers, 2 marks in total**)
3) cheer you up (**1 mark**)
4) E.g. happily (**1 mark**)

Page 21 — Summary Questions

1) Tobi feeds a lamb for the first time. — 5
Tobi arrives at the farm and remembers the past. — 2
Tobi enters the barn and meets the lamb. — 4
Tobi's reaction to being given an important responsibility. — 6
Tobi's first impressions of the cottage. — 3
(**1 mark for all correct**)
2) things can be better than you expect (**1 mark**)

Page 21 — Compar

1) E.g. At first he doesn't like the farm and is unhappy about having to stay there, but later he enjoys his stay. (**1 mark**)

Section 3 – Theseus and the Minotaur

Pages 26-27 — Fact Retrieval Questions

1) every nine years (**1 mark**)
2) fourteen (**1 mark**)
3) two (**1 mark**)
4) sandy beaches (**1 mark**)
AND
distant mountains (**1 mark**)
5) attend a feast (**1 mark**)
6) Daedalus (**1 mark**)
7) She could return to Athens with him. (**1 mark**)
AND
She could become his wife. (**1 mark**)
8) a) snores (**1 mark**)
b) eyes (**1 mark**)
9) E.g. He threw himself between the Minotaur's legs. (**1 mark**)
OR
E.g. Theseus dived forwards and slid between the Minotaur's legs. He then killed the Minotaur from behind. (**2 marks**)
OR
E.g. He was inspired to dive forwards and slide between the Minotaur's legs. This confused the Minotaur, so Theseus could jump up behind it and kill it. (**3 marks**)
10) E.g. He followed the thread back to the entrance. (**1 mark**)
OR
E.g. He had unravelled the thread as he was walking through the maze. This meant he could follow the thread back to the entrance. (**2 marks**)

Pages 28-29 — Inference Questions

1) In a time long before any living person can remember (**1 mark**)
2) It tells you they were feeling nervous. (**1 mark**)
3) They were stripped of their weapons.
The entrance was sealed shut.
They were plunged into darkness.
(**1 mark for any of the above answers**)
4) He had the ball of thread.
He had hidden a sword under his tunic.
(**1 mark for any of the above answers**)
5) E.g. The Minotaur has "sharp, pointed horns". (**1 mark**)
OR
E.g. The Minotaur is described as being a "formidable size" and having "sharp, pointed horns" (**2 marks**).
6) heavy (**1 mark**)
7) E.g. So no-one in the town would see them and report their escape. (**1 mark**)

Fiction

8) E.g. Theseus wants to stop the Minotaur from harming his people. (**1 mark**)
OR
E.g. Theseus puts his own life in danger to kill the Minotaur, because he wants to stop it from harming other people. (**2 marks**)
OR
E.g. Theseus volunteers to stop the Minotaur to help his people, even though it is dangerous. He helps Ariadne by letting her leave with him, so that her father won't punish her. (**3 marks**)

Page 30 — Word Meaning Questions

1) E.g. fear (**1 mark**)
2) thankful (**1 mark**)
3) cautiously (**1 mark**)
4) confused (**1 mark**)
5) reassuring (**1 mark**)

Page 31 — Summary Question

1) Theseus leads Ariadne and the other tributes to safety. — 6
Theseus sees the Minotaur for the first time. — 4
A dangerous fight begins. — 5
Ariadne offers help to Theseus. — 3
Theseus and the other tributes travel to Crete. — 2
(**1 mark for all correct**)

Page 31 — Structure Question

1) action — Theseus dived sideways
past events — The Minotaur had been imprisoned for years
setting — sandy beaches and distant mountains
character — Crete's cruel king, Minos
(**1 mark for all correct**)

Section 4 – Flight

Pages 36-37 — Fact Retrieval Questions

1) rode her bike around the local park
watched television
(**1 mark for any of the above answers**)
2) She felt a tugging in her back. (**1 mark**)
3) b) (**1 mark**)
4) her mum (**1 mark**)
5) She knocked over a lamp. (**1 mark**)
6) She was going to get a glass of water. (**1 mark**)
7) the top of a hill (**1 mark**)
8) the farmland (**1 mark**)
9) sheep — in the fields
otters — in the river
hawk — in the sky OR in the clouds
(**1 mark for any of the above answers, 3 marks in total**)
10) She chose a soft patch of grass. (**1 mark**)
AND
She pulled her wings in slowly. (**1 mark**)

Pages 38-39 — Inference Questions

1) It says they fly "high above the rooftops".
It says they make shapes in the air while flying in formation.
It says their wings are sleek/streamlined/graceful/powerful.
Amina seems to be impressed by the birds — it says she "admired" them.
(**1 mark for any of the above answers**)
2) She tried to keep the pain from her voice. (**1 mark**)
3) a) Amina (**1 mark**)
b) They paused in their bleating.
They gazed up.
(**1 mark for any of the above answers**)
4) It didn't want to share its space in the sky with Amina.
It tried to make Amina move away.
(**1 mark for any of the above answers**)
5) She stayed close to the farm animals instead of going back up to the clouds. (**1 mark**)
6) sunrise (**1 mark**)
7) She "crept" in through the back door. (**1 mark**)
8) E.g. shocked (**1 mark**)
OR
E.g. I think she felt shocked, because she was "wide-eyed" and dropped the mug. (**2 marks**)
9) E.g. She was breathless with excitement. (**1 mark**)
OR
E.g. She was "in awe" of her wings when she got them, and she "whooped with delight" when flying over the river. (**2 marks**)
OR
E.g. When she first got her wings, she was "in awe", and she was "breathless with excitement" when she tried flying for the first time. She also "whooped with delight" when flying over the river. (**3 marks**)

Page 40 — Word Meaning Questions

1) scratching (**1 mark**)
2) calm (**1 mark**)
3) E.g. tiny (**1 mark**)
4) She was falling fast.
She was falling steeply.
(**1 mark for any of the above answers**)

Page 41 — Summary Questions

1) Amina's life before she got wings (**1 mark**)
2) Amina uses her wings to fly around. (**1 mark**)

Page 41 — Language Question

1) E.g. To show that she was in a rush to get back. (**1 mark**)

Non-Fiction

N.B. An 'E.g.' before an answer means that it's just a suggestion.
For questions which ask for an opinion, interpretation or explanation, there won't always be one 'correct' answer. Pupils' answers to these questions may vary from the answers we've suggested, but they should give a similar amount of detail, and should always be based on the text.

Non-Fiction

Section 1 – Frozen Escapes

Pages 6-7 — Fact Retrieval Questions

1) basic conveniences
warm rooms
comfortable beds
the promise of a good night's sleep
(**1 mark for any of the above answers, 2 marks in total**)
2) Sweden (**1 mark**)
3) snow and ice (**1 mark**)
4) To make the most of the winter season.
So they can take paying guests for as long as possible.
(**1 mark for any of the above answers**)
5) It takes time to plan the construction of an ice hotel.
(**1 mark**)
6) polar bears
a fairy-tale carriage
(**1 mark for both correct**)
7) She's too busy to notice. (**1 mark**)
8) attend an ice sculpting workshop
steam in a sauna
soak in a hot tub
(**1 mark for any of the above answers, 2 marks in total**)
9) Marvin Okoye — is a magazine reporter
Johanna Burgess — is an expert on the tourism industry
Kevin Vernet — is a student from France
(**1 mark for all correct**)

Pages 8-9 — Inference Questions

1) It says they go the extra mile for their guests.
It says they try to give their guests an experience that's out of the ordinary.
(**1 mark for any of the above answers**)
2) Because ice is cold.
Because ice is wet.
Because ice is uncomfortable to sleep on.
Because ice melts in warm temperatures.
(**1 mark for any of the above answers**)
3) E.g. She likes ice hotels. (**1 mark**)
OR
E.g. I think she finds ice hotels exciting, because she says it's "thrilling" to stay in one. (**2 marks**)
4) Most artists who apply are rejected. (**1 mark**)
5) Because it's an experience like no other. (**1 mark**)
6) Carrie Tollington is from Essex. — Fact
Staying in an ice hotel is a fun experience. — Opinion
You can try skiing at many ice hotels. — Fact
Outdoor winter pursuits are boring. — Opinion
(**1 mark for all correct**)
7) Because they are hot, so you can warm up from the cold temperature of the ice hotel. (**1 mark**)
8) E.g. He feels enthusiastic. (**1 mark**)
OR
E.g. I think he feels enthusiastic about ice hotels, because he says they're "fantastic". (**2 marks**)

Page 10 — Word Meaning Questions

1) short (**1 mark**)
2) E.g. trustworthy (**1 mark**)
3) E.g. It's unlike any other environment. (**1 mark**)
4) idea (**1 mark**)

Page 11 — Summary Questions

1) Constructing ice hotels (**1 mark**)
2) E.g. There are many indoor and outdoor activities that you can try when you stay in ice hotels. (**1 mark**)

Page 11 — Language Question

1) E.g. That they're beautiful.
That they're amazing.
That they're unusual.
That they're like something from another world.
That they look as if they were made by magic
(**1 mark for any of the above answers, 2 marks in total**)

Section 2 – Loggerhead Sea Turtles

Pages 16-17 — Fact Retrieval Questions

1) Because their heads are unusually large. (**1 mark**)
2) around a metre (**1 mark**)
3) every few minutes (**1 mark**)
4) a) seaweed (**1 mark**)
b) jellyfish
crabs
other shellfish
(**1 mark for any of the above answers**)
5) around 60 days (**1 mark**)
6) moonlight (reflected on the ocean's surface)
the moon
(**1 mark for any of the above answers**)
7) Human developments put them off leaving the sea.
Sea defences can destroy their nesting sites.
(**1 mark for both correct**)

Non-Fiction

8) They get caught in fishing nets, which can injure or kill them.
They collide with boats or propellers.
They often mistake rubbish in the sea for food.
(**1 mark for any of the above answers, 3 marks in total**)

Pages 18-19 — Inference Questions

1) They saw the fall of the dinosaurs.
They saw the rise of human civilisation.
(**1 mark for any of the above answers**)
2) an opinion (**1 mark**)
3) They can travel to many parts of the world.
They can swim hundreds or even thousands of miles.
(**1 mark for any of the above answers**)
4) They return to the beach they hatched on, even though they might not have been there for decades. (**1 mark**)
5) fight their way out of the eggs (**1 mark**)
6) to avoid predators (**1 mark**)
7) It says that light from roads and buildings can disorientate them.
It says that they are at risk from predators.
It says that they can face man-made hazards.
(**1 mark for any of the above answers, 2 marks in total**)
8) E.g. Because loggerhead sea turtles eat jellyfish. (**1 mark**)
OR
E.g. Loggerhead sea turtles eat jellyfish, so they are likely to eat plastic bags by accident, because they think they are jellyfish. (**2 marks**)
9) E.g. It makes them feel hopeful. (**1 mark**)
OR
E.g. It makes them feel worried, because it says that they are still "in grave danger". (**2 marks**)

Page 20 — Word Meaning Questions

1) avoid (**1 mark**)
2) E.g. It includes lots of different things. (**1 mark**)
3) shelter (**1 mark**)
4) E.g. serious (**1 mark**)

Page 21 — Summary Question

1) How and where baby loggerhead sea turtles hatch. — 4
How artificial light affects baby loggerhead sea turtles. — 5
The swimming and navigating skills of loggerheads. — 3
The issue of plastic bags in the sea. — 6
The breathing habits and diet of loggerhead sea turtles. — 2
(**1 mark for all correct**)

Page 21 — Prediction Question

1) E.g. Worse, because the female loggerhead sea turtles are finding it much harder to lay their eggs. (**1 mark**)
OR
E.g. Better, because people are trying to help the baby loggerhead sea turtles get to the sea. There are also projects to stop dangerous rubbish getting into the sea. (**2 marks**)
OR
E.g. Worse, because they face lots of dangers, such as being caught in fishing nets which injure or kill them, or accidentally eating plastic bags. They also face dangers on land, such as their nesting sites being destroyed. (**3 marks**)

Section 3 – International Fireworks Contest

Pages 26-27 — Fact Retrieval Questions

1) once a year
every October
(**1 mark for any of the above answers**)
2) France (**1 mark**)
3) Each team's display lasts thirty minutes. — False
Spectators don't have to pay to watch the contest. — True
The USA, China and Ireland regularly take part. — True
A team from the UK is competing in this year's contest. — False
(**1 mark for all correct**)
4) a) two pupils from Loweton Primary School (**1 mark**)
b) They won the 'Photograph a Firework' competition. (**1 mark**)
5) pop music (**1 mark**)
AND
classical music (**1 mark**)
6) People coming from all over the country for the contest. (**1 mark**)
7) They're not big enough.
They quickly overflow.
(**1 mark for any of the above answers**)
8) They are advised to arrive early to avoid the queues.
They are advised to walk or to take public transport rather than drive.
(**1 mark for any of the above answers, 2 marks in total**)

Pages 28-29 — Inference Questions

1) Thousands of people went to the park to watch the first night (**1 mark**)
2) There are rides to keep children entertained before the fireworks. (**1 mark**)
3) Fireworks displays should be very colourful. — Opinion
The music for the displays is always amazing. — Opinion
Canada performed first during this year's event. — Fact
Canada won the competition last year. — Fact
(**1 mark for all correct**)

Non-Fiction

4) It says that people think Canada's display is "the one to beat".
   It says Canada set off the largest number of fireworks ever used in a display at the contest.
   It says the music was provided by two very famous opera singers.
   (**1 mark for any of the above answers, 2 marks in total**)
5) Bethany Cawfield says she had to put her hands over her ears. (**1 mark**)
6) E.g. Anna Riley likes the competition. (**1 mark**)
   OR
   E.g. Anna Riley really likes the contest. She says she has been "every year since the contest began" and is "always one of the first to arrive". (**2 marks**)
7) flooded by a sea of rubbish (**1 mark**)
8) It says the weather is "expected to be fair" for the rest of the contest.
   It says that you can "meet the teams" on two days.
   It says that there will be a "special celebration" on Sunday.
   It says that there's "plenty of excitement on offer".
   It says that Bulgaria will use "novel techniques that have never been seen before".
   (**1 mark for any of the above answers, 2 marks in total**)

Page 30 — Word Meaning Questions

1) impress (**1 mark**)
2) E.g. thrown away (**1 mark**)
3) found solutions to the Environment Society's worries (**1 mark**)
4) assist (**1 mark**)

Page 31 — Summary Questions

1) the fireworks contest in Loweton (**1 mark**)
2) Fireworks displays are really exciting. (**1 mark**)

Page 31 — Comparison Question

1) E.g. This year, the weather was clear and dry, but in previous years, the weather has been really bad. (**1 mark**)

Section 4 – The Real Blackbeard

Pages 36-37 — Fact Retrieval Questions

1) Edward Teach (**1 mark**)
2) 1717 (**1 mark**)
3) the Queen Anne's Revenge (**1 mark**)
4) food
   wine
   silk
   weapons
   (**1 mark for any of the above answers, 2 marks in total**)
5) the Caribbean
   the coast of America
   (**1 mark for both correct**)
6) It was lost after it ran aground. (**1 mark**)
7) He would get a pardon for his crimes.
   He would be able to attack ships without being punished.
   He would share his spoils with the state governor.
   (**1 mark for any of the above answers, 2 marks in total**)
8) Blackbeard worked for the British navy. — True
   Blackbeard's fleet had a crew of 40 men. — False
   Farm owners wanted to help Blackbeard. — False
   Blackbeard was killed in November 1718. — True
   (**1 mark for all correct**)
9) E.g. He ambushed Blackbeard. (**1 mark**)
   OR
   E.g. Some of Maynard's crew hid. When Blackbeard boarded the ship, they came out and attacked him. (**2 marks**)
   OR
   E.g. Maynard ordered some of his crew to hide below decks. This made the ship look empty, so Blackbeard thought it was safe to board it. Maynard and his men then jumped out and ambushed Blackbeard. (**3 marks**)

Pages 38-39 — Inference Questions

1) an opinion (**1 mark**)
2) is believed to have been (**1 mark**)
3) E.g. They would have felt scared of him. (**1 mark**)
   OR
   E.g. They would have been afraid of him, because he looked like a "demonic creature". (**2 marks**)
4) Blackbeard demanded a chest of medicines as a ransom for his hostages. (**1 mark**)
5) It says that Blackbeard was "True to his word".
   It says that Blackbeard released the prisoners when the medicines were delivered.
   (**1 mark for any of the above answers**)
6) E.g. It meant he didn't need to kill anyone to take over ships. (**1 mark**)
   OR
   E.g. It made people really scared of him. This meant he could take over their ships "using terror alone", without killing anyone. (**2 marks**)

Non-Fiction / Poetry

7) clever (**1 mark**)
8) E.g. No, because the writer says the rumours of Blackbeard's treasure have "little basis in fact". (**1 mark**)
9) E.g. Yes, because he attacked ships. (**1 mark**)
OR
E.g. No, because he released the prisoners from Charleston Harbour without hurting them, and some historians think he never killed anyone. (**2 marks**)

Page 40 — Word Meaning Questions

1) menacing (**1 mark**)
2) E.g. became known as (**1 mark**)
3) It's famous for being a bad thing. (**1 mark**)
4) E.g. captured (**1 mark**)
5) inquisitive (**1 mark**)

Page 41 — Summary Questions

1) Details about Blackbeard's appearance. — 3
The discovery of a shipwreck and its contents. — 6
The early years of Blackbeard's pirate career. — 2
Blackbeard's actions in Charleston Harbour. — 4
The events that led to the death of Blackbeard. — 5
(**1 mark for all correct**)
2) the life and times of a pirate (**1 mark**)

Page 41 — Structure Question

1) E.g. The first paragraph introduces the "legend" of Blackbeard, and the last paragraph says more might be learnt about his "legend". (**1 mark**)

N.B. An 'E.g.' before an answer means that it's just a suggestion.
For questions which ask for an opinion, interpretation or explanation, there won't always be one 'correct' answer. Pupils' answers to these questions may vary from the answers we've suggested, but they should give a similar amount of detail, and should always be based on the text.

Poetry

The Great Fire

Page 4 — Fact Retrieval Questions

1) 1666 (**1 mark**)
2) in the middle of the night (**1 mark**)
3) tables
chairs
beds
sheets
(**1 mark for any of the above answers, 2 marks in total**)
4) The fire spread through narrow passageways. — True
The wind stopped the fire from spreading quickly. — False
It had rained a lot in the summer before the fire. — False
People went onto the Thames to escape the fire. — True
(**1 mark for all correct**)
5) E.g. The City must be rebuilt. (**1 mark**)

Page 5 — Inference Questions

1) stating a fact (**1 mark**)
2) On them the fire leaps greedily (**1 mark**)
3) E.g. He was wearing his nightgown. (**1 mark**)
4) a) E.g. It got rid of the "deadly poisons" left over from the Black Death. (**1 mark**)
b) E.g. Because thousands of people's homes had been burnt down. (**1 mark**)

Page 6 — Word Meaning Questions

1) E.g. They moved quickly. (**1 mark**)
2) ablaze (**1 mark**)
3) E.g. orders (**1 mark**)
4) reduce (**1 mark**)

Page 7 — Summary Question

1) A description of the fire happening. (**1 mark**)

Page 7 — Comparison Questions

1) E.g. Before his command, the fire was burning all over the city, while afterwards, it gradually went out. (**1 mark**)

Poetry

2) E.g. During the fire, they felt scared and panicked. After the fire, they felt hopeless. (**1 mark**)
OR
E.g. The fire caused "fear and panic" — Londoners were scared during the fire. After the fire, they felt hopeless because "Thousands" of houses had burnt down. (**2 marks**)

Journey

Page 10 — Fact Retrieval Questions

1) one (**1 mark**)
2) for a long time (**1 mark**)
3) green (**1 mark**)
4) roads
city lights
(**1 mark for both correct**)

Page 11 — Inference Questions

1) Mountains are flattened to mounds (**1 mark**)
2) It has no rivers.
It's dry.
(**1 mark for any of the above answers)**
3) E.g. The narrator can see small things, such as "a boy in a tree". (**1 mark**)
4) A continent spanned — (**1 mark**)
5) The narrator says it's a "fabulous land". (**1 mark**)

Page 12 — Word Meaning Questions

1) grasp (**1 mark**)
AND
grip (**1 mark**)
2) snatched (**1 mark**)
3) shone (**1 mark**)
4) Got smaller (**1 mark**)

Page 13 — Summary Questions

1) the plane taking off (**1 mark**)
2) from a city, over beaches and mountains, to a different city (**1 mark**)

Page 13 — Language Question

1) E.g. It's big.
It's scary.
It's unnatural.
It's unfriendly.
(**1 mark for any appropriate answer, 2 marks in total**)

The Dragons Are Hiding

Page 16 — Fact Retrieval Questions

1) on horseback (**1 mark**)
2) to show they were brave (**1 mark**)
3) Dragon hunters looked for treasure. — True
Dragon hunters worked in groups. — False
Dragon hunters needed to have good eyesight. — True
Dragons would eat during the day. — False
(**1 mark for all correct**)
4) Scotland (**1 mark**)
AND
Wales (**1 mark**)

Page 17 — Inference Questions

1) an opinion (**1 mark**)
2) E.g. A lick of their flame could "paralyse" someone. (**1 mark**)
3) didn't want to fight dragon hunters (**1 mark**)
4) E.g. Their sounds can be "disguised" by waterfalls. (**1 mark**)
OR
E.g. Their wings are very quiet, and the places they live in are "secret". (**2 marks**)
OR
E.g. The sounds they make are hard to hear, such as "the whisper of wing-beats". You also have to look in unusual places, such as "mineshafts", and might have to "dig" to find the dragons sleeping. (**3 marks**)

Page 18 — Word Meaning Questions

1) complete (**1 mark**)
2) cunning (**1 mark**)
3) They couldn't be found. (**1 mark**)
4) abandoned (**1 mark**)

Page 19 — Summary Question

1) The narrator gives advice to young dragon hunters. — 4
The countryside makes the narrator think about dragons. — 5
Signs of dragons have been reported again. — 3
The narrator describes what it was like to hunt dragons. — 2
(**1 mark for all correct**)

Page 19 — Prediction Question

1) E.g. No, because they haven't been found since they disappeared. (**1 mark**)
OR
E.g. Yes, because the narrator finds it "easy to believe" that dragons might be found again. I think the recent "rumours" will help people to find them again. (**2 marks**)
OR
E.g. No, because dragons haven't been seen for "a very long time", and all the trails of them have "proved cold". The "rumours" might just be the sounds of things like thunder and waterfalls. (**3 marks**)

Poetry

The Battle

Page 22 — Fact Retrieval Questions

1) seagulls screeching
   small dogs yapping
   (**1 mark for any of the above answers)**
2) seven o'clock (**1 mark**)
3) b) (**1 mark**)
4) white (**1 mark**)
5) They tried to rebuild the castle.
   They tried to bail water out of the castle.
   (**1 mark for any of the above answers)**

Page 23 — Inference Questions

1) It is very hot.
   The sun is "blazing".
   There are people sunbathing.
   Children are eating ice-creams.
   (**1 mark for any of the above answers)**
2) worried (**1 mark**)
3) The moat was dug around it quickly.
   The windows could be carved with one swish of a hand.
   (**1 mark for any of the above answers)**
4) For a while we admired our glorious creation (**1 mark**)
5) The army "consumed" the castle.
   The army tore down the castle walls.
   The army caused the tower to crumble.
   The army knocked the flag into the water.
   (**1 mark for any of the above answers, 2 marks in total**)

Page 24 — Word Meaning Questions

1) E.g. It tells you they moved quickly. (**1 mark**)
2) convinced (**1 mark**)
3) assault (**1 mark**)
4) sadly (**1 mark**)
5) victorious (**1 mark**)

Page 25 — Structure Questions

1) The castle moat is created. — 3
   The enemy army reaches the castle door. — 4
   The flag falls off the castle. — 5
   The sun sets. — 6
   A warning is given about the high tide. — 2
   (**1 mark for all correct**)
2) Then the starting gun sounded with a roar of the ocean
   (**1 mark**)

Page 25 — Prediction Question

1) E.g. I think they will rebuild the sandcastle. (**1 mark**)
   OR
   E.g. They will rebuild the sandcastle. The army believe the castle "could not rise again" but the group think this is an "error". (**2 marks**)

Velvet Dresses

Page 28 — Fact Retrieval Questions

1) hills, cliffs, roads (**1 mark**)
2) fossils (**1 mark**)
3) Dorset's countryside is brown and red. — False
   The narrator compares fields to teeth. — False
   The narrator wants to walk through woods. — True
   Dorset's soil has a lot of clay in it. — True
   (**1 mark for all correct**)
4) Africa (**1 mark**)

Page 29 — Inference Questions

1) like a patchwork quilt, stained
   yet stitched with years of love
   (**1 mark for any of the above answers**)
2) E.g. It suggests that the narrator wants to explore every part of Dorset. (**1 mark**)
3) steep and varied (**1 mark**)
4) The narrator wants Dorset's history to be part of their identity. (**1 mark**)
5) welcoming (**1 mark**)

Page 30 — Word Meaning Questions

1) big (**1 mark**)
2) E.g. They are rocky (**1 mark**)
3) E.g. spread out (**1 mark**)
4) run (**1 mark**)
5) blend (**1 mark**)

Page 31 — Summary Questions

1) The narrator imagines exploring Dorset. (**1 mark**)
2) They love Dorset and want to feel they belong there. (**1 mark**)

Page 31 — Language Questions

1) E.g. It is a cosy, comforting place. (**1 mark**)
2) E.g. It makes them sound lush and beautiful. (**1 mark**)

Poetry

The Frost

Page 34 — Fact Retrieval Questions

1) loud (**1 mark**)
2) The Frost avoids travelling through valleys. — False
The Frost travels to a train station. — False
The Frost expects to be busy. — True
After he visits the trees, the Frost flies west. — True
(**1 mark for all correct**)
3) E.g. To make people think about the fact that they had forgotten to prepare for him. (**1 mark**)
4) burst it in three (**1 mark**)

Page 35 — Inference Questions

1) He whispers about his plans.
He decides to go "out of sight".
He decides to go "In silence".
He doesn't want to travel with the other types of weather.
(**1 mark for any of the above answers**)
2) He protects it. (**1 mark**)
3) He moved over the windows "like a fairy".
He "crept" over the window panes.
(**1 mark for any of the above answers**)
4) E.g. He creates lots of different pictures out of frost. (**1 mark**)
OR
E.g. He uses his imagination to create frost pictures of interesting things, such as "cities with temples and towers".
(**2 marks**)

Page 36 — Word Meaning Questions

1) quivering (**1 mark**)
2) They are around the edges of the lake. (**1 mark**)
3) There are lots of them.
They are all close together.
(**1 mark for any of the above answers**)
4) E.g. expensive (**1 mark**)

Page 37 — Summary Questions

1) The Frost makes a decision and travels to different places.
(**1 mark**)
2) Frost can affect lots of different things. (**1 mark**)

Page 37 — Language Question

1) E.g. They are hard.
They are shiny.
They are valuable.
They are beautiful.
They reflect the light.
They are transparent.
(**1 mark for any appropriate answer, 2 marks in total**)

1219 - 19988

Serving Suggestion:
Delicious with fresh chives

ISBN 978 1 78294 837 7
9 781782 948377

E6HRA22
£2.00
(Retail Price)

www.cgpbooks.co.uk